b

Martin, Philip J T
3 A bone flute : poems / Philip Martin. Canberra : Australian National University Press, 1974.
63 p. ; 22 cm.
Includes bibliographical references.

I. Title.
PR9619.3.M28B6 821 74-76817
Information Design + 483/1375 MARC

A Bone Flute

A Bone Flute

Poems Philip Martin

Australian National University Press Canberra 1974

First published in Australia 1974

Printed in Australia for the Australian National University Press, Canberra

North, South, and Central America: International Scholarly Book Services, Inc., Portland, Oregon

ISBN 0 7081 0465 7

Library of Congress Catalog Card no. 74-76817

Published with the assistance of the Literature Board of the Australian Council for the Arts

Acknowledgements

Grateful acknowledgements are due to:

The Age
Australian Poetry
Poet's Choice
Quadrant
Times Literary Supplement
Australian Broadcasting Commission

Contents

3

I

Death-Gift

A Sequence

In one place lay
Feathers and dust, today and yesterday.

John Donne

Emblem

for Alec King

Where at Nicaea the palace of Constantine
Once stood, and now a bare tree spreads its branches
Over a few stones by violet water,

A grader lately pushing earth aside
Sank to a vaulted tomb. Sunlight discovered
Grief outweighed: paintings on every wall

Still fresh in greens and reds and ripe wheat colour.
On the far wall two peacocks,
Emblems of immortality, between them

An urn brimming green the waters of heaven,
And on the floor below, a heap of bones
Blent by pyre and time to the wall's yellow.

One composition: the mortal shards resigned,
The long necked peacocks, tails furled, at their urn
Sipping forever.

The Bog People

1 *A Young Girl*

Two thousand years ago
They brought this girl out here and staked her down
At knee and elbow, seeing the gods required it.

Hurried back to their huts.
Night was rising from the bog, spreading from the dense
Trees outward, closing the space of the fens.

They left her cries to lessen
In the night thickening down upon her
As the peat afterwards which held her close,

For the archaeologist
To uncover now, tell us the colour of the hair,
Show us how intricately she has it braided.

'Charming', he breathes, alive
To the living of the dead.

The Bog People

2 *'But if a living dance upon dead minds*
why, it is love' (e.e. cummings)

For it's a live scholar
Who leans to the bog's lip,
To the tanned features, the body's
Diminishing curve into sleep,
Brown-over-brown, relief.
Gently to be removed to a museum,
Studied, for life.

Or no scholar but an earlier man,
Peasant with a spade
Struck still this overcast May afternoon.
He calls the village priest,
Then, as he's told, buries the dead once more,
Shivers the vision off with straightening back,
And turns with unaccountably light step
Away towards home,
The steaming broth of evening. Wife-warmed to sleep.

Cairo Museum

'Cooch Noomberr Two, look!
All this are what the Pharaohs
Took with them into the Second World.'

The Egyptian guide,
Grey-robed, elderly, tall,
Trying to focus the touristic gape.

Here by the phials of liquid,
The wheat, the young king's sandals,
His pectoral on which the holy scarab

(Chalcedony, translucent)
Pushes the boat that bears
The one eye of eternal life,

I see, lit by the phrase,
What these dead meant:
Not this world and another

But a procession.
From the First World, all this,
Into the Second.

Newgrange, Ireland

The centuries of grass have covered them.
The mound, a door, a passage into the dark.
Here the dead were a stone saucer of ashes.
Corbels kept them from the rains of Meath.
They brought with them no gold to break this darkness,
But stone, stone objects only.

Yet a lost mathematics planned
Light's ritual visitation. Over the door
A slit: midwinter morning,
For seventeen minutes of the year the sun
Stoops, travels the long curved passage, swings
Around the chamber where it would call upon
The dead among their death-gifts.

This morning, lit by the same beam, a scholar
Stands in the swept place: plunderers were here,
And what breath blew the ashes from the dish?
Light returns to the mound, the voided room,
The centuries in grass grow over them.

Another Emblem

for Patrick McCaughey

That fountain in Rome, crowning its narrow street,
A convent school beside it. From a distance
Under its canopy, sienna-brown,
It's a low altar with three candles, closer
Proves a sarcophagus.
Pagan figures look out under the brim
Through lapse of time as water,
A woman's head, the features smoothed away,
A countryman or god
With a ram slung on his shoulders. Up from the place
Where first the body lay,
Rectangular hollow washed and washed in light
To liquid alabaster wavering green,
Three jets constantly leap, and where they spill,
Out of the shadowy archway children pour
Into the middle of day.

Tongues

The speaker is a woman whose husband has died
after a long illness

Three days before he died the hospital called me:
He was unconscious, sinking. I went at once.
His face was closed, remote against the pillows.
I sat by the window. The leaves outside were moving.
Suddenly he began to speak. I thought
He was asking me for something, but before
I could cross the room I saw how fixed his eyes were,
And then realised: he was speaking verse,
But in a language neither of us knew.
Not English certainly, not German, and not Russian,
His family's language from the thirteenth century,
Though he had never learnt it.
                                        He continued
For a full minute, measured, authoritative.
I picked up the rhythm: four stresses to each line.
I recall only the opening words of one:
Alléndam tatsú . . .
                                He seemed to be speaking
Past me, his eyes directed to the window,
Yet also to me. For thirty lines or more
He spoke, and then, as if the poem was finished,
Fell silent and lay back.
                                    Two hours after,
He spoke once more, in German, using my name.
His eyes were softened and again familiar.
We did not refer to the poem, then or later.
But though he was conscious almost until he died
He took no leave of me. And I think now
The poem was his taking-leave.

His doctor,
Who speaks German fluently, believes
That what I heard was German, much distorted.
I am certain it was not: the voice was too
Distinct, unfaltering.
His father said,
'Ah yes. Of course I need not remind you, we
Are an old family. It was our forebears speaking.'

Roman Bird-flute

'Well: this is a flute,'
The learned Dutchman tells us.
'It has been found in Hulland
In a Roman tomb. It belonged
Let's say to a Roman soldier
Who reached this point at the end
Of the Imperium Romanum.
He probably died (he's dead now)
And he took his flute with him
In the barrial-place.

Well:
What's the material?
Of course, it is a bone.
The wing-bone of a vulture.
(Perhaps the gryphon vulture.)
The bird-flute is about
Twellev inches long
And has six holes. I find
Its voice akin to the voice
Of a hobo. No, an oboe
(A hobo, that's a tramp):
The oboe tune?' 'Timbre?'
'Timbre. Thank you.

So:
I suppose it is now the moment
To blow. To make it speak.
It is varry difficult, but
If you have pesshunce . . .'

He blows. He makes it speak.
His live lips carve a tune

Where once the Roman's did
On a wing-bone of the death-bird:
Piercing from the bone
Sharp as a beak
Till the breath fails.

Wayside Tombstones, Jugoslavia

They stand by remote
Upland roads, are known
To the rare traveller,
To home-winds and winds
That have crossed frontiers.

Seldom a body
Rotting beneath the headstone.
Over the primitive, strong lunged
Chanting of wind
The stone accents ride,

'Serbian red brightened
A foreign mud. I died
Far from here, for freedom.
And not sorry for it,
Not sorry for it,
Not sorry.'

Tombs of the Hetaerae

after Rilke

—

In their long hair they lie, and with their brown
Faces gone deep into themselves, their eyes
As if in front of too much distance closed.
Skeletons, mouths, flowers. And in their mouths
The smooth teeth set in ivory rows
Like pocket chessmen. Flowers, beads, slender bones,
Hands that lie on a dress of fading weave
Over the heart, a building fallen in.
But there under those rings and talismans
And eyeblue stones (so many favourites' keepsakes)
The silent crypt of sex
Standing unruined, brimmed to the vault with petals.
Yellowing pearls, unstrung and rolled apart,
Bowls of baked earth adorned under the lip
With the painted beauties of their mistresses,
Green shards of unguent-vases smelling of flowers,
And little gods, and household altars showing
Delighted gods in heavens of hetaerae.
Gold clasps, and metal belts that seem burst open,
Scarabs, small figures of gigantic sex,
A laughing mouth, shapes of runners, of dancers,
Amulets, crockery, ornamental pins.
And again flowers, and pearls rolled far apart,
The bright loins of a small lyre, and between
Veils falling below the knee like mists,
As if it crept from the chrysalis of the shoe,
As light as air the ankle's butterfly.

So they lie filled with things,
With precious stones and toys and bric-à-brac,
With broken tinsel (all that fell into them),
Darkening like the bottom of a river.

And riverbeds they were.
Over them and away in swift waves pressing
On to the next life and the next, the next,
The bodies of many youths rushed in a torrent,
And the full rivers of men.
And sometimes boys broke from their childhood mountains
And came down in a hesitating fall,
Played with the things on the riverbed until
The fall and its momentum seized them. Then
They filled the expanse of this broad watercourse
With clear, still-shallow water, eddying
Where it grew deep, for the first time reflecting
The banks, the distant birdcalls, while above them
The starred nights were a heaven that nowhere closed.

Such riverbeds they were.

Among long hair they lie, brown faces secret,
The crypt of sex now barred with funeral petals,
The precious eyes now closed on too much distance.

Monteverdi: *The Coronation of Poppea*

A joy like sorrowing.
The sound of arches.

Where has this gravity, this
Severe tenderness gone
Out of the Italians?

Seventy-five.
At the end of your leave-taking
Nero and Poppea
Have murdered and intrigued
Their way into each other's arms.
No trace
Of guilt. They sing
'My beloved'
'My beloved'
held in a calm rapture,
'I adore you'
'I adore you'.

What does this mean
From you, on the lip of the grave?

Doctor Donne of Paul's: the Statue Jack Built

for Joanne Lee Dow

This survived the fire that ruined the church
Where when the love-songs stopped he preached the sermons
To which all London flocked. The statue rises
Out of the painting he himself commissioned.
He got from his deathbed, climbed into his shroud,
'Paint me like this', he ordered.

It's very witty, a friend said, go and see it.
Now as I stand beneath, some guide explains,
'Towards the end, of course, he grew quite morbid.'
I can't let that pass, give her a short lecture.
What does she make of that last hymn, in fever,
'I joy, to see my west'?

Morbid at the end? Then morbid ever,
Lovers parted were always, for him, dead worlds,
Even together they died (but rose the same).
Death weighs upon his eyeballs now. And yet
The beard and the moustache are somehow jaunty,
The shroud's tucked at the head

To the shape of a small crown. What style he had,
Not merely enduring what he must
But playing as he went. An actor first,
Wearing his Melancholy Lover's hat
Black and extravagant, an actor last,
Great visitor of ladies,

Great frequenter of plays, and very neat,
Now after the many nights he showed
His masculine persuasive force, his centric
Happiness concentric unto Her,
He folds his hands over his genitals,
Closing them for the night.

Sir Thomas Browne, Physician of Norwich

for Sir Clive Fitts and Adrian Serong,
Physicians of Melbourne

The great tomb-haunter. Here, near the Cathedral,
The area still marked in the rush of traffic
'Tombland' prompts me again to summon you.

In this town, back from Padua and Leyden,
You saw your patients steadily, good physician,
Found vision in the doctor's common round,

Caring, curing, and, past cure, resigning
To 'the mighty nations of the dead, since every hour
You know adds to that dark society'.

A literary doctor, committing to paper
(As to their lives, their deaths, the bodies you treated)
A doctor's Credo, curious, whimsical

Almost as much as sonorous. Though some,
Reading you now, claim you toy with your subject,
I am not one of them, and least of all

When the burial urns come into your hands. What music
You bring to archaeology, what knowledge
Of custom, at once delighted in and questioned,

When your voice sounds in these sad pitchers, echoes
In the marble vault built everywhere, your spirit
Probing diversities: the body dissolves

In Innocents' Churchyard, keeps in the sands of Egypt,
Yet it's all one. The flourishing calm of Norwich
In one live century was bank and shoal

Enough for the meditation to wind out
Through all time, past the bed of Cleopatra
From which no skill calls up the ghost of a rose,

Space, too, for you to look, near midnight,
Through Norfolk panes at stars as huge above
Low fields as in the Antipodes, and know

That it was time to close the ports of knowledge:
In the New World, huntsmen were up already.
Time and space to reflect, turning to sleep,

That 'sleep itself must end, and as some conjecture'
(Believer doubting in the margin there)
'All shall awake again.' Accept this fee,

Doctor, maker of that instrument
Which resonates the motions of a brain
Feeling gravely in time the pulse of death.

2

Poet

after Rilke

You are leaving me, unhesitating hour,
Your wings bruise me with flight.
Alone, what purpose shall I find my mouth?
My night? My day?

No love to share my house, no house to share,
Where I might say, I live.
All things to which I give and give myself
Grow rich and squander me.

Stroke of Midnight

after Pierre Reverdy

All is extinguished
The wind sings past
Trees shiver
All animals are dead
No-one is left
See
The stars no longer shine
The earth stops turning
A head bends
Its hair sweeping the night
From the last tower left standing
Clangs the hour

Deserted Homestead

for Doreen Breen

The wind
Like those who built here strikes
In from the sea,
Fingers the hewn sandstone,
Frets and scoops it.

Inside
Where lives branched, a tree
Marks with the trunk's curve
The angle of two walls, reaches
Arms into emptied space.

A bird
Whose nest is elsewhere
Flies the passages
Crying
An alien life.

Anima-figure

for Heather Formaini

I knew her as a friend before
She moved in with him and lost
Character name and face.
Now in his flat but keeping up her own
In case he leaves for Denmark or Japan,
'I'm living a double life', she said today.
No, not even a single life,
And little sign she's guessed. Yeats wrote that some
Must never hope for wholeness of the self
But hollow out their hearts, consent to be
The lamp that holds another's wick and oil.
Is her state what he meant?
I speak to her and wonder if she hears,
But not me only, no voice gets to her,
As if she had un-learnt that words, beings,
Not forgetting her own, might have a meaning.
His face, because of her, fills out,
Grows to the image that it wills itself,
Hers, blind, at a standstill,
Is less itself than ever I have seen it,
No longer hers, unable to be his,
Less even than a mask for hers or his.

The War is Not Over

for Henry and Winifred Nowottny

Edge Hill. Battle once joined stays joined,
Our echoes roll, the noise of battle rolls
From soul to soul, yes, and through the senses
Of men now, with ears quick to the dead.

At Edge Hill, on the ridge where I am staying,
The King's army drew up, at dawn struck down
On Cromwell's men below. Now, each October,
The locals hear it, English grinding on English,
Hear the trampling of horses on the wind,
Clashing of swords, guns, the gnash of chains.

My hosts' son, at college, tells his parents
A dubious tale, perhaps: The B.B.C.
Set tape-recorders listening in the woods;
From a high frequency the sounds, played back,
Paled the technicians: out of the muddy roar,
Not to be doubted, human voices shrieking.
Too horrible to use. The tapes were wiped.

Ronsard to Hélène

When age brings you to meagre fire and candle
And you sit winding, spinning the thread at evening,
Musing my lines aloud you'll say 'Ronsard
When I was beautiful sang me to fame'.
No drowsy serving-maid will fail to stir
Hearing that legend.

                    I will be under earth
Less than a voice grown still among the shadows
And you a web-skinned crone hunched at the fire.
You will regret you gave me scorn for love.

Live, let my living voice persuade you. Now
While there are roses, pluck them.

A Summer Woman

Summer has come to this city of canals,
Its northern clime assumes a southern weather
She had forgotten, muffled in clothes: now,
Days and warm days insisting, throw them off.
Beyond the half-drawn curtains a church lifts
Its Dutch tower into Mediterranean blue,
In the half-darkened room she is walking naked.
And more than hair she loosens the whole body,
Walking from room to room, her bare feet knowing
Ridges of matting, the very grain of timber,
The body the being itself expanding to
This amplitude on either side the fabric
Swaying across the windows. Under them
A boat swishes past in a pause of traffic,
Bells high in the tower spangle noon air.
She walks, held by her room beyond constriction,
Alone, greeting a lover.

Sea-child

She was born of a wave seen from a headland
On a blue morning through a boy's held gaze,
Or from still higher, some divinity flying
Who sees white born and vanish in the blue
And is not satisfied and makes a wish,
Godlike, itself the act. However seen,
White born of the blue she comes to land,
And not as a wave. She steps ashore unbreaking,
Her birthplace in her eyes.

To a Visiting Poet

Before you arrived, the blackness.
Power gone, I could not lift a finger
For self, parent or friend.

At the first glimpse I knew that I should like you,
Found in your shape and face, your voice, your questions,
Lines of your origins,

The origins of your lines
That earlier sounded me, that dragged my waters,
A dark net in their darkness.

Morning, I wake to find you out already
In winter stillness washed and shining as spring.
But, more than this, it is your simplicities

Restore to my soul its motions.
A bird darts from the bushes
To blue air, I can bless once more,

Move in space and self with arms extended
To touch the world with fingertips once more
Reverent, find myself tuned

To a music from far back, ancestral, as
Your face, in Australia now, utters distinctly
Past currents of change the Europe of its features.

Credo

after Kazys Bradunas

I believe in the end,
In the ebbing-out of the blood
Late in autumn,
In the quiet of the grave.
I believe in the beginning,
In the flying of the birds
In early spring,
Far off in eternity.

[with Julia Gylys]

Reflection

for Joseph O'Dwyer

My image in the window, night beyond.
Looking up from the page, I see it in
Too dark a glass to show what time is doing;
But mine, reflection of this solid being.
Strange that it's there at all, and strange in how
Few years even that outline will be gone.
As when the light returns outside, tomorrow.

Poem

for A. D. Hope

'Spend life to house old bones'

A man alone, aware of his aloneness,
Of being in this like all men, watching the sun
Descend into the hills beyond the sea
And night come, takes a pen and writes his poem,
The words whatever they say
Saying 'I have been here. Remember me.'

Spend life to house old bones? No, but their flesh,
The night-breeze fluttering papers to the floor,
Cars on the highway like a voice. Not 'Mourn',
'Remember' he is saying. 'Find in me
Your self who never found me.
For this is breath housed in the stone flowered urn.'

About This Woman

About this woman
With hair making the sunlight tangible
Summer flows in and centres,

As in more sombre decor
Dusk concentrates in cypresses or round
The sole tower in a landscape,

Or in some myth the river
Gathers its shapeless flow to a nymph's form
That stands and wades ashore.

Twisting like braided hair
Light liquefied pale amber into this flask
The wine of summer pours.

Man to Woman

You lean above me,
Your hair in the dark
Pours down over us both.

Beneath its flood
Buoyant, undrowning
I swim upward towards you.

You move upon me
As wind upon a landscape
Bending and working.

As you bear down
I rise, and the sap in me,
As a tree into the night.

After

1

The house is not demolished,
Nor have we left it. Only
The east wing is closed.

At times through its locked doors
A music drifts to us,

Eyes behind the eyes
Trace from those windows
The line of hills at dawn,
Soles of the feet recover
The cool of floorboards.

2

This is the known
Way of a ghost: midwinter,
In a closed room,
A perfume out of nowhere.
The cheek is kissed.

3

In tossing dark
A briar catches the sleeve,
Touch of lost fingers.

We are far inland.
The wave of a dried sea
Breaks over us.

From an Unknown European Poet

Disappeared and so
Seeming dissolved
Essence dispersed in water

You are gone into this wind
That blows back to me this evening
Almost the body of that breath
This wind stirring the air about me
A scarf you've worn sweeping against my face

Though you are gone into
The great belittling spaces of the world
Into my own recesses

These clouds tonight travelling east renew me
There is some sister of yours to be encountered
I have no home now gladly
Such clouds freighted with light deepening the night sky
It is more than the city's light they carry

An Encounter

Through a room dense with talk you first approach.
You are dressed simply in purple, you have run
Mauve lights through your fair hair, your face
Shapes a severity, medieval-modern.
Your English carries an accent, slight, your own.
But I can't tell at times if what you say
Is cliché, or something you feel deeply
And can't express as yours. Yet you can say
'Wisdom' or 'dignity' without pretension.
I can't weigh you. Can't even guess your age:
Thirty?
            You say, 'I am learning pottery.
It is good exercise of the whole body,
And more than body. I have made, and put away,
An imaginary figure.'
                        'What sort of figure?'
'A male figure. I admire physical beauty,
Female, male.'
                You praise it till I say,
'I value it too, but I don't let myself
Think of it too much' (seeing my own stocks dwindle).
Gravely, considerately, you ask,
'An accident? Have you, perhaps, a scar?'
(At least on this point I can reassure you.)

Separate together among these fifty others,
We seem, I seem, to move in a dimension
New but remembered from another time,
With another of your race.
                            But watching the light
Fall on the fine veins beside your eyes
I feel as I have never felt: a woman,

Under the gaze of a man. Some sense in you
Is searching me, as a hand feels this way and that
In earth where coins are buried.

Walking at midnight
On windy grass, a rediscovered power
In body and more than body lifts my arms
Towards the hurrying sky: a new beginning.

3

A Bottle of Arpège

This gift you'll wear, do not mistake its meaning.
It is a breath, of course, but not the air
That you sing, living: it is a grace-note merely,
And in your syntax,
In the eloquence of a given day or night,
Merely an adjective one might dispense with.
But you, my love, the noun and the strong verb.

Fruits of Experience

A dish of apples: two are large and smooth,
The third smaller. Its skin, my fingers learn,
Has just begun to wrinkle. So I choose it:
The fruit inside is likely to be sweeter.

Fish

In these sand-shallows
This hushed sun-haze morning
One fish small as a minnow
Darts and is still

At rest the colour of sand
Now it no longer is
Only now when it moves
Again a flick of being

From Greece

1 *Click-clacks in Athens*

for Peter Levi, S.J.

A new craze here this summer
Two balls on a string
That click like castanets
Tat tat tat tat
Faster closer to frenzy
It's like machine-gun fire

Under the Acropolis
Tonight in a narrow street
It closes in, the clacking
Rockets from wall to wall to wall and back
Tat tat tat tat
Tatteta tatteta tatteta tat

2 *Epiphany*

for Paul Kovesi

On a mountain road
Driving from Dodona
The holy place you stop
For goats
Streaming down from the rocks.
After the last one crosses
A girl appears, coming
Towards the car. She says
Nothing but reaches
In through the open window,
Touches the steering-wheel,
Touches your hand.

In a Coffee-shop

At the next table I see
Them gravely talking, then
Silent, gaze within gaze.
She draws his eyes down, slips
The gold ring from her finger.

Scenes from Sexual Life

At Puberty

The first flow of blood, the first of seed:
Pray for the right parents.

Impulse

She is just twenty. Across the room she sees
One man among the many, and is seen.
She crosses the room, she speaks, it all begins.

In Love

Tonight's cold wind can't touch me: you have touched me.

Crux

Let them be utterly virgin till they marry,
Then, before knowledge, marry until death.

Wife

No matter how we began (and it was well,
That fast embrace), each morning now I wake
At my edge of the bed.

Divorcee

She's wild, they said of me.
I married a tame husband,
And mild and wild spun outward.
The second time, they tell me,
You marry your first mistake.
Let's see. This man is gentle,
We wind each other in.

Leipzig, 1729

Two Poems on Bach

1

Good Friday, *The Passion according to Saint Matthew.*
Eccentric, monstrously long. Some there remembered
The things he'd done to that well-loved old hymn
'Dear God, when will I die?' No reverence.
The boys' light voices, woodwinds totally
Unconcerned, he'd made it frivolous.
Now
As twilight closed on the church and he turned homeward
He heard, as he was meant, the well-set-up
Frau Blank exclaim, 'Why, it was comic opera.'
Parts put away, the work had served, was finished,
And no one played it for a hundred years.

2

How does it look from 1970?
The great Handel, on tour, is passing through.
Sebastian Bach, the humble organist,
His kind of art already out of fashion,
Writes, 'A brief interview would be an honour.'
Handel hasn't the time.

Petrarch's Crown

Young, my brother and I
Went to enormous lengths
Crisping and curling our hair,
Three times a week with the tongs
We did, outdid, each other.

Years later as I marched
Through thronging streets to receive
The laurel wreath, some woman
Tipped from an upstairs window
A vile brew on my head.

Since when, under the laurel
Not a hair will grow.
I have triumphed, yes, throughout
My world I am a legend.
The smooth crown irks me, though.

Offensive Language

for Rob Liersch

'A New Zealand youth who called two policemen
"pigs" was ordered to spend a day in a piggery.'

News Item

I admit it. I was wrong.
I'd just spelt it out on the wall
NIXON IS ROSEMARY'S BABY
When the Boys rolled up. Wit, no,
But quite sharp with the elbow.
You pigs, I said. The judge
Said, Off with him to the pig-sty,
It'll teach him a lesson.
Right!
Can't say I took to the smell,
But the creatures themselves: so grateful
For all that we set before them
And a pink doze in the sun.
It just wouldn't do to compare
This with life at the station.
Another time, I'll choose
My words with a bit more care.

British Goldfish

I came to the courtyard
With gold leaves wavering down
Through warm air to the paving.
The fish in the pond swam glowing,
Easy, lazy.

I came next
When snow iced the paving.
The pond was frozen hard.
Alas, I said, poor goldfish,
They must be stone-dead, surely.

Now, six days later,
The courtyard stones are dry,
The pool changed back to water,
And fish, fish again swimming
Gold and easy.

Not dead, they simply waited
Glowing under the ice
Until the siege was lifted.
True British goldfish, these
Could take it, they survive.

Bequest

To those who never read, I leave my writings,
Just what they never wanted, tunes for the deaf,
Skywriting for the blind. To plagiarists,
A style, if not the taste for it. To critics,
Pushing aside their flagons to despatch
The work of half a life in half an hour,
This Christian hope: May they not wake in Limbo
Blushing. To the politicians of my birthplace
Who, not being God, do not provide: in time
Of drought, a cup of muddy water. And
To my coolest mistress, my electric blanket.

Notes

The Bog People

Those buried, usually after sacrificial killing, in peat-bogs in Denmark, and in many other parts of northern Europe. The most widely known of these is the Tollund Man, uncovered by peat-diggers in 1950. The noble and tranquil head, under its small cap, is tanned by bog-water and almost sculptured in appearance. My details for these poems come from *The Bog People* by P. V. Glob (London, Paladin Books, 1971).

Newgrange, Ireland

A large burial mound, with others nearby, on a hill above the river Boyne in County Meath. The origin of those who built it, perhaps 4,500 years ago, is still uncertain. The poem was suggested by a visit to the mound and by Claire O'Kelly's *Guide to Newgrange* (Wexford, John English, 1971). It was her husband who discovered the date on which light enters the vault. Standing inside with the door sealed, he observed that the vault was 'dramatically illuminated' and that many details, such as the corbels, were clearly seen.
Corbels: stones fitted together without mortar to form a beehive-shaped vaulting.
Meath: pronounced to rhyme with *breathe.*

Wayside Tombstones, Jugoslavia

Adapted from the feature *Krajputasi* (Roadside Tombstones), produced by Radio Belgrade.

Tombs of the Hetaerae

Hetaerae: courtesans of the ancient world. In adapting this poem from Rilke's *Neue Gedichte* I have left a few lines untranslated, condensed one or two others and spelt out an implied image. The last four lines are my own but are made up of material from the original.
Hilary Appleby has helped me greatly but the liberties taken are my responsibility, not hers.

Doctor Donne of Paul's: the Statue Jack Built

Donne himself distinguished between 'Jack Donne' and 'Doctor Donne', his earlier and later selves. Izaak Walton in his *Life* of Donne describes the making of the portrait during the last days of Donne's life. On this picture was based the marble effigy in St. Paul's, London, which was the work of a sculptor with the highly appropriate name of Stone.
The poem, besides quoting and misquoting from Donne's own words, echoes a well-known description of him as a young man: 'not dissolute but very neat, a great visitor of ladies, a great frequenter of plays, a great writer of conceited verses'.

Sir Thomas Browne, Physician of Norwich

Browne's prose writings quoted or paraphrased here are: *Letter to a friend upon occasion of the death of his intimate friend*, *Religio Medici*, *Urne Buriall* and *The Garden of Cyrus* (all to be found in the Everyman selection from his works).

Anima-figure

'I remember the case of a girl of about fifteen . . . She would not go to school or submit to any kind of discipline . . . An older man of some prominence in the artistic world was in love with her and the girl thought of herself as his inspiration and his guardian angel . . . The artist actually did find inspiration from his association with her. This might be all very well for the artist, but it was bound to spell ruin for a girl in such a position. For, instead of going on with her own education and development, she was reduced to being nothing but a psychological function of the man. She was limited to being his "soul", just as Eve was for Adam, instead of taking up her own task of becoming an individual woman in her own right.'

(M. Esther Harding, *The Way of All Women*, London, Rider & Company, 1971, page 25.)

Versions from French, German and Lithuanian

I am grateful to a number of people for their help: in particular, to Roland and Julia Husson, Dennis Davison, René Gold, James McCaughey, Enid Neal and, above all, Julia Gylys (the poem from Kazys Bradunas is as much her work as mine) and Hilary Appleby.

Designed by ANU Graphic Design/Adrian Young MSIA
Set in 11 point Monotype Joanna one point leaded
and printed on 89 gsm Old Vale Antique
at The Griffin Press, Netley, South Australia